Turning Point Battles
of the Civil War

Sandra J. Hiller

CRABTREE
Publishing Company
www.crabtreebooks.com

UNDERSTANDING
THE CIVIL WAR

Author: Sandra J. Hiller
Publishing plan research and development:
  Sean Charlebois, Reagan Miller
  Crabtree Publishing Company
Editors: Mark Cheatham, Kirsten Holm, Lynn Peppas
Proofreader: Wendy Scavuzzo
Editorial director: Kathy Middleton
Production coordinator: Shivi Sharma
Creative director: Arka Roy Chaudhary
Design: Sandy Kent
Cover design: Samara Parent
Photo research: Iti Shrotriya
Maps: Paul Brinkdopke
Production coordinator: Margaret Amy Salter
Prepress technician: Margaret Amy Salter
Print coordinator: Katherine Berti

Written, developed, and produced by Planman Technologies

Photographs and Reproductions
Front cover: © Blue Lantern Studio/Corbis; Title Page: Library of Congress (top); The Granger Collection, New York (bottom); Table of Contents (p. 3): Bettmann/CORBIS, Chapter 2: Library of Congress, Chapter 3: North Wind / North Wind Picture Archives, Chapter 4: The Granger Collection, New York, Chapter 5: Library of Congress. Chapter Opener image (pp. 5, 11, 19, 20, 37): Mary Evans Picture Library/Photolibrary
Bettmann/CORBIS: pp. 6, 24, 37; CORBIS: pp. 4, 31; Eon Images: pp. 25, 42; The Granger Collection, New York: pp. 28, 32; Ken Welsh/Photolibrary: p. 16; Library of Congress: pp. 7, 8, 9, 15 (top and bottom), 17, 22, 26, 27, 30, 38, 39, 40, 41; Mary Evans Picture Library/Photolibrary: p. 12; North Wind / North Wind Picture Archives: pp. 13, 21; North Wind Picture Archives / Alamy: p. 14; Universal History Archive/Photolibrary: p. 43

Front cover: General George Pickett leads the charge at the Battle of Gettysburg.
Back cover (background): A military map of the United States from 1862 shows forts and military posts.
Back cover (logo): A civil war era cannon stands in front of the flag from Fort Sumter.
Title page (top): Soldiers' National Cemetery at Gettysburg
Title page (bottom): Lincoln's address at the dedication of the Soldiers' National Cemetery at Gettysburg, November 19, 1863

Library and Archives Canada Cataloguing in Publication

Hiller, Sandra J., 1956-
    Turning-point battles of the Civil War / Sandra J. Hiller.

(Understanding the Civil War)
Includes index.
Issued also in electronic formats.
ISBN 978-0-7787-5343-8 (bound).--ISBN 978-0-7787-5360-5 (pbk.)

    1. United States--History--Civil War, 1861-1865--Campaigns--
Juvenile literature. I. Title. II. Series: Understanding the Civil War

E470.H55 2011   j973.7'3   C2011-907492-3

Library of Congress Cataloging-in-Publication Data

Hiller, Sandra J., 1956-
  Turning point battles of the Civil War / Sandra J. Hiller.
      p. cm. -- (Understanding the Civil War)
  Includes index.
  ISBN 978-0-7787-5343-8 (reinforced library binding : alk. paper) --
ISBN 978-0-7787-5360-5 (pbk. : alk. paper) -- ISBN 978-1-4271-9942-3
(electronic pdf) -- ISBN 978-1-4271-9951-5 (electronic html)
  1. United States--History--Civil War, 1861-1865--Campaigns--Juvenile
literature. I. Title.
  E470.H65 2011
  973.7'3--dc23
                                        2011045084

Crabtree Publishing Company

Printed in the U.S.A./082019/PS20190710

www.crabtreebooks.com   1-800-387-7650

Published in Canada
Crabtree Publishing
616 Welland Ave.
St. Catharines, Ontario
L2M 5V6

Published in the United States
Crabtree Publishing
PMB 59051
350 Fifth Avenue, 59th Floor
New York, New York 10118

Published in the United Kingdom
Crabtree Publishing
Maritime House
Basin Road North, Hove
BN41 1WR

Published in Australia
Crabtree Publishing
Unit 3 – 5
Currumbin Court
Capalaba QLD 4157

TABLE *of* CONTENTS

> *We are met on a great battlefield. . . . We have come to dedicate a portion of that field as a final resting-place for those who here gave their lives that [our] nation might live. . . . The world will little note nor long remember what we say here, but it can never forget what they did here.*
>
> —Abraham Lincoln, Gettysburg Address, November 19, 1863

The Twentieth Maine regiment at the Battle of Gettysburg, July 2, 1863

Introduction

When the Civil War began in April of 1861, both the Union and the Confederacy entered the conflict with excitement. Each side expected to quickly defeat the other side in a short, glorious battle. Sixteen months later, the realities of war had shocked both sides.

The Reality of War

By the fall of 1862, both sides were badly battered. The South had won most of the major battles but at a terrible cost. As 1862 moved into 1863, victory seemed to seesaw between the two sides. Six major battles from September 1862 to November 1863 were turning points in the war.

After the First Battle of Manassas, or Bull Run as it was called in the North, both sides began to prepare for a long struggle. Governments in the North and the South began to **mobilize**, equip, train, and effectively use their armies. They needed raw materials, factories, experienced officers, and good organization. The South had a strong military tradition and excellent officers. The North had the **resources** and manpower to fight a long war.

"War at the best is terrible, and this war of ours, in its magnitude and in its duration, is one of the most terrible."

—Abraham Lincoln

Major Events
1862

June 25–July 1
Seven Days Battles

August 29–30
Second Battle of Manassas

September 17
Antietam

✶ What Do You Know!

Shoddy was a cheap, recycled wool fabric. Northern factories made uniforms out of shoddy. Since the fabric did not hold up well, the word was soon used to describe anything that was poorly made or fell apart when used.

Goals of War

The North entered the war with one goal: to preserve the Union. The common view in the North was that **secession** was illegal and the Confederate states were in rebellion. The rebellion had to be put down to preserve the Union. The Southern states, on the other hand, were fighting for state's rights and to preserve their slave-based economy. As long as battles were fought in the South, Confederate soldiers were fighting for their homes.

As the war progressed, Southern slaves provided labor for the Confederate war effort. Slaves worked the fields while their masters fought. By July of 1862, Lincoln had decided that **abolition** was an important military goal. Abolition changed the focus of the war. When the Union's goals included ending slavery, foreign nations such as England and France were less likely to support the South.

The Emancipation Proclamation

Abraham Lincoln actually wrote the **Emancipation Proclamation** in July 1862, but he set it aside to wait for a Union victory. It was two months

President Lincoln and his cabinet working on the Emancipation Proclamation

before the opportunity arrived. On September 22, 1862, following the Battle of Antietam, the Emancipation Proclamation was issued. The Proclamation warned the Southern states that, if they did not stop fighting and return to the Union by January 1, 1863, their slaves would "be then, thenceforward, and forever free." The final proclamation was issued on January 1, 1863. It was a military action and applied only to slaves in areas fighting against the Union. Slavery in states fighting on the Union side could only be addressed by the legislature.

George B. McClellan

One of President Lincoln's greatest difficulties as commander-in-chief was finding the right general to lead the war effort. After the First Battle of Manassas in July 1861, President Lincoln asked General George B. McClellan to handle the task of turning new **recruits** into soldiers. McClellan was good at this job. Lincoln promoted him to general-in-chief in November 1861. When it was time to put his men into battle, however, McClellan was indecisive. He overestimated the enemy's strength and spent too much time getting his army in order instead of getting it into the field.

General George B. McClellan

Finally, in the summer of 1862, Lincoln named General Henry Halleck general-in-chief, leaving McClellan as general of the Army of the Potomac. John Pope was put in charge of the new Army of Virginia. Pope was given

McClellan *"has the Army with him. . . . We must use what tools we have. There is no man in the Army who can lick these troops of ours into shape half as well as he . . . If he can't fight himself, he excels in making others ready to fight."*

—Abraham Lincoln

the task of defending Washington, DC, and the Shenandoah Valley, which had been part of the job of McClellan and the Army of the Potomac.

General John Pope led the Union forces in the Second Battle of Manassas. Unfortunately for the Union, he was as unsuccessful as McClellan. He made poor decisions and he missed opportunities to press weak points in the Confederate lines. The battle ended in another Union retreat. In fact, Pope's leadership was so poor that he made even McClellan look good. Pope was removed and his Army of Virginia was folded into McClellan's Army of the Potomac. Lincoln based his decision on the fact that the soldiers respected McClellan. The army's reaction proved that Lincoln had made the right decision. The soldiers **responded** to McClellan and, within days, he had turned a defeated force into a battle-ready army.

Robert E. Lee

While the Union was still searching for a strong military leader, the Confederacy had found one in Robert E. Lee. The first year of fighting brought General Lee into a position of leadership in the Confederacy's military. Lee was born in Virginia and was a graduate of West Point. When the Civil War began, he resigned his position in the United States Army and joined the Confederate army.

In June of 1862, Lee was placed in command of the Confederate army

General Robert E. Lee (center)

cautious and weak under grave responsibility . . . likely to be timid and irresolute in action.

—George McClellan, about Robert E. Lee

in Virginia. Unlike McClellan, Lee took the offensive in battle. He was not afraid to launch daring attacks even when his army was outnumbered. Under his skillful leadership, the Confederates were victorious in the Seven Days and Second Manassas battles. As a military **strategist**, Lee believed that the South could win the war only if the war could be carried into the North. This is why he launched two major attacks in Union territory.

Marching to Maryland

When the Second Battle of Manassas ended, Lee's army had the victory but little else. The army was tired, poorly fed, and lacked basic supplies. Lee could not stay at Manassas because the agricultural land around him was destroyed by war. There were not enough **provisions** (food and supplies) for his men and horses. Besides, he wanted to stay on the **offensive**.

Lee decided to move forward into Maryland. This answered several of Lee's concerns. His army would **forage** for provisions in Union territory. He would be in a position to threaten the Union capital, Washington, DC. The Union troops, he thought, would still be disorganized and discouraged from the Second Battle of Manassas. Finally, he believed that the slaveholders of Maryland would welcome his troops. Unfortunately, Lee did not know that McClellan had brought the army back to fighting strength. In addition, he was entering a part of Maryland that was **sympathetic** to the Union cause.

Special Orders 191

One more event worked against Lee's plans for Maryland. On September 13, two Union soldiers found a copy of Lee's plans for the invasion of Maryland. The paper, Lee's Special Orders 191, was carelessly mislaid by a Southern officer. With Lee's plans in McClellan's

People in the War

General Henry W. Halleck

General Henry Halleck, called "Old Brains," was put in command of the Union's Western forces early in the war. His field commanders won a number of victories including Fort Donelson, Fort Henry, Pea Ridge, and Shiloh. In July 1862, he was made General-in-Chief of Union armies and moved to Washington, DC. It was generally thought that Halleck was a good administrator but a terrible field commander. He did not do well in his role as General-in-Chief. He was widely disliked in Washington due to his inability to give clear orders or to take responsibility. At one point, President Lincoln described Halleck as ". . . little more . . . than a first-rate clerk."

Before the war, Halleck was a California lawyer and businessman. He helped to author the California state constitution. He was also the author of a textbook on military tactics.

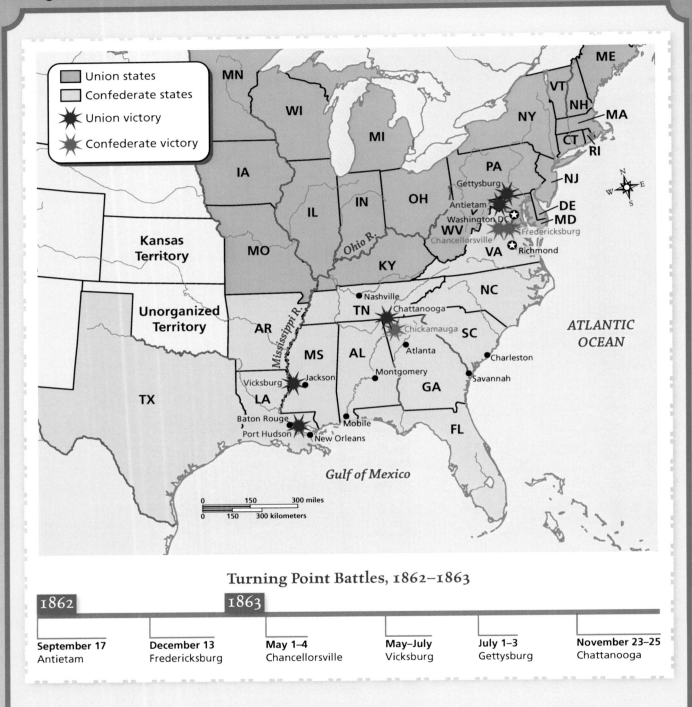

Turning Point Battles, 1862–1863

1862		1863			
September 17 Antietam	December 13 Fredericksburg	May 1–4 Chancellorsville	May–July Vicksburg	July 1–3 Gettysburg	November 23–25 Chattanooga

hands, the element of surprise was gone. By mid-September 1862, the stage was set and the **principal** players were moving into position for their meeting at Antietam. The battle at Antietam would be a turning point in the Civil War.

Battles at Antietam and Fredericksburg

General Lee and his army crossed the Potomac River on September 4, 1862. In the border state of Maryland, Lee counted on support from slaveholding citizens. He also believed that the Union Army of the Potomac was too disorganized and broken from the Second Battle of Manassas to threaten him. He soon discovered that he was wrong on both counts.

Antietam

For his plan to work, Lee needed to safeguard his supply line to the south. This required that his troops capture the Union garrison at Harper's Ferry. With his supply line **secure**, he could move into the heart of Union territory. Lee divided his army into four sections. The largest section was sent to capture Harper's Ferry. He expected his divided army to join up again before General McClellan and the Union army could cross South Mountain and attack.

. . . if we defeat the army arrayed before us, the rebellion is crushed, for I do not believe they can organize another army. But if we . . . meet with defeat, our country is at their mercy.

—George McClellan, before the Battle of Antietam

Major Events

1862

August 29–30
Second Battle of Manassas

September 4
Lee enters Maryland

September 17
Battle of Antietam

November 7
General Burnside replaces McClellan

December 13
Battle of Fredericksburg

Lee's plans were no longer secret, however. McClellan's men had found the paper showing Lee's plans to divide his army and the path that each group was to take. McClellan did not move quickly to attack Lee before his forces rejoined. Instead, McClellan spent time organizing his forces. In the meantime, a spy informed Lee of the danger, and Lee was able to reassemble his army before McClellan arrived. Lee sent forces to block McClellan at South Mountain. Confederate troops engaged the Union army on September 14. They slowed, but did not stop, the Union advance. Union forces also failed to reach Harper's Ferry before it fell into Confederate hands the next day.

Since Lee had lost the element of surprise, he considered whether to retreat or stay and fight. News of the Confederate victory at Harper's Ferry encouraged Lee to stay. He positioned his army on high ground near Antietam Creek outside Sharpsburg, Maryland. Lee still expected to meet a weakened enemy in battle.

The Army of the Potomac gathered on the east side of Antietam Creek. The Union army outnumbered the Confederate forces almost 2 to 1 but, as usual, McClellan was convinced that he was facing a stronger enemy. He hesitated to attack and, while he hesitated, more **reinforcements** from Harper's Ferry arrived to fill out Lee's army.

General George McClellan and his troops at the Battle of Antietam

The Battle

On September 15 and 16, the two armies marched into position and prepared for battle. They finally engaged on September 17. McClellan planned to begin the attack on Lee's left, which was held by Confederate General Jackson. When he thought the time was right, he would attack on the right and advance in the center.

Battle of Antietam

The battle began at dawn and lasted 12 dreadful hours. The Union attack on Lee's left flank was met with a determined defense. At the center, Union troops pierced Lee's line but failed to follow up on their advantage. On the right, General Ambrose Burnside took an important bridge over Antietam Creek but then delayed two hours before moving forward. By then, the Confederate troops in front of him had been reinforced by more troops from Harper's Ferry.

McClellan's army greatly outnumbered Lee's, but McClellan did not take advantage of this. McClellan held more than one-quarter of his men in reserve. His failure to coordinate attacks and use his entire army allowed Lee to move men around the battlefield and meet threats one at a time.

The next day, September 18, both forces regrouped and buried their dead. That night, Lee's army left Maryland. McClellan, still afraid of being outnumbered, did not pursue and attack the retreating army. There was no clear winner at Antietam but, since Lee withdrew, the Union celebrated it as a victory. Lincoln issued the Emancipation Proclamation on September 22. With this announcement, the Union added freedom for slaves to the goal of preserving the Union.

> ### What Do You Know!
>
> Like the nation, West Point was divided by the Civil War. West Point graduates commanded in 60 Civil War battles. In 55 of these, West Point graduates faced one another across the battlefield. Thomas J. "Stonewall" Jackson and George B. McClellan both graduated from West Point in the Class of 1846.

President Lincoln issued the Emancipation Proclamation after the Union victory at Antietam. This picture shows freed slaves reaching Union lines.

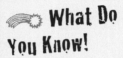 **What Do You Know!**

Uniforms are important! When the Civil War began, various state militias had their own uniforms. Soldiers did not always know who was a friend and who was an enemy. Sometimes men were mistaken for enemy soldiers and killed by friendly fire. At other times, enemies were allowed to approach too closely because they looked like friendly forces.

Outcome of the Battle

Antietam was the single bloodiest day in American military history. The total number of **casualties** for the Union and Confederate armies together was close to 23,000. This number includes the dead, the wounded, and the missing or captured. Battlefield photographers documented the scene immediately after the battle. Their work provided a lasting record of the death and destruction at Antietam.

After the Battle of Antietam, Lincoln ordered McClellan to pursue the weakened Confederate army. McClellan, however, insisted that he lacked supplies and organization. His delays allowed Lee to regroup and protect Richmond, the capital of the Confederacy. This delay caused Lincoln to finally remove McClellan from command. On November 7, McClellan was replaced by General Ambrose Burnside. Just over a month later, December 11–15, Burnside commanded the Army of the Potomac at the Battle of Fredericksburg, another turning point of the war.

The Battle of Fredericksburg

The Battle of Fredericksburg, in Virginia, was among the largest and deadliest battles of the Civil War. It included a river crossing under fire, street-to-street fighting, and the unsuccessful assault of strongly-held Confederate positions. It was also a stunning defeat for the Union.

The Plan

General Burnside's plan was to cross the Rappahannock River and take the war to Richmond. Until his troops reached the Rappahannock River, he had speed and surprise on his side. At the river, however, his plans began to fall apart. The flat-bottomed boats needed to build bridges across the river had not yet arrived. Instead of changing his plans, Burnside ordered the army to wait. This delay gave Lee a week in which to bring his army to Fredericksburg and arrange his men in strong and defensible positions. Confederate riflemen set up sniper positions in waterfront homes and buildings. From there, they could fire at Union engineers when construction of the bridges finally began on December 11.

Carrying Out the Plan

Burnside had three bridges built downstream from the town, and these were completed under cover fire from Union **artillery**. At Fredericksburg, however, rifle fire from **snipers** in the town made construction of the

> *my loyalty is growing weak. … I am sick and tired of disaster and the fools that bring disaster upon us. …*
>
> —Union soldier, after the Battle of Fredericksburg

People in the War

Mathew Brady

When the Civil War began, Mathew Brady was already a well-known portrait photographer. Only a portion of the Civil War photographs connected with him were actually made by him, but it was his idea to train and fund a team of photographers who traveled with the Union army. He and his staff documented all aspects of army life, including the battlefields before the dead were removed. Through his work, people far from the war were exposed to its horrors.

Union forces crossing the Rappahannock River during the Battle of Fredericksburg

General Burnside (right) ordering General Hooker to charge Marye's Heights at the Battle of Fredericksburg

bridges there impossible. Finally, three regiments of the Union army crossed by boat to take care of the Confederate riflemen. The riflemen did not give up their ground easily and heavy house-to-house fighting raged through the town.

Once across the river, Burnside's plan was to use part of his force against Lee's southern flank while the rest of the army held back Confederate troops on Marye's Heights. This plan, like so many before and after, was spoiled by poor leadership and missed opportunities. To begin with, time was lost when the Union forces stopped to **plunder** the town on December 12. In the fighting on December 13, Union soldiers made early progress, but their generals failed to send in reinforcements to support them. Above all, thousands of lives were lost due to poor decisions by Union generals.

To understand the battle of Fredericksburg, it helps to compare the Civil War with previous wars. In previous wars, large numbers of soldiers and cavalry faced one another across the battlefield. The soldier's weapon was a musket, which had a limited range and was not particularly accurate. A direct assault on a **fortified** position could be effective. The rifle was a new and better infantry gun used in the Civil War. Rifling, or spiral lines inside the barrel, improved the accuracy of the weapon at great distances. Rifle fire from an entrenched position was deadly.

> *It can hardly be in human nature for men to show more valor, or generals to manifest less judgment.*
>
> —Newspaper report on the battle for Marye's Heights

At Marye's Heights, the Confederates occupied a sunken road protected by a stone wall. Union forces had to advance over about 400 yards (366 m) of open ground to reach the Confederate lines. They were exposed to a rain of rifle fire. Using the old methods of attack, Union officers ordered wave after wave of soldiers to directly assault the Confederate position. Thousands of men were cut down before the stone wall.

> *If there is a worse place than Hell, I am in it.*
>
> —President Lincoln, following the battle at Fredericksburg

Outcome of the Battle of Fredericksburg

In the end, the Army of the Potomac suffered 12,600 casualties. Almost two-thirds of these were at Marye's Heights. On the other hand, the Confederates lost less than half that number, about 5,300 men.

The Battle of Fredericksburg was more than a devastating Union loss. It was a humiliating retreat. Burnside withdrew his army under cover of darkness the night of December 15. Soldiers were disheartened by

Confederate troops fighting from behind the stone wall at Marye's Heights at the Battle of Fredericksburg

the waste of lives. They questioned the wisdom and intelligence of their leaders. Both Burnside and Lincoln were harshly **criticized**. The weeks following the Union loss at Fredericksburg were among the darkest for the Union.

Although Fredericksburg was a victory for the Confederacy, it was an empty victory. Lee's army was still hungry, tired, and poorly fed. The victory did nothing to solve the pressing problems of feeding an army in a countryside destroyed by fighting. Even though the Confederate Army lost fewer than half the men lost by the Union, the Confederacy could not replace its losses.

Two Turning Points

Both the Battle of Antietam and the Battle of Fredericksburg were turning point battles in the Civil War. Antietam, in spite of heavy casualties on both sides, was a Union victory. The Confederates had brought the war into Union territory and had been driven back across the Potomac River. Even though the battle at Fredericksburg returned **momentum** to the Confederates, the battle was fought in the South. The next two turning point battles were mirror images of the first two: Chancellorsville was another empty victory for the South and Gettysburg was a final attempt to take the war into Union territory.

3 Chancellorsville and Gettysburg

The disaster at Fredericksburg was the end of General Burnside's short career as commander of the Army of the Potomac. Burnside accepted responsibility for the loss, but the public and Congress also blamed President Lincoln.

Between Fredericksburg and Chancellorsville

Armies usually did little or no **campaigning** in winter because of poor weather and road conditions. To compensate for the failure at Fredericksburg, however, Burnside tried to stage a January campaign. Dry weather gave way to heavy rain as Burnside's army began marching in January 1863. Roads turned to mud, and men, mules, and artillery pieces could not move. The "Mud March" forced Burnside to cancel the winter campaign.

Following this second disaster, President Lincoln removed General Burnside as commander of the Army of the Potomac. General Joseph

Major Events
1863

January 26
General Hooker replaces Burnside

May 2–6
Battle of Chancellorsville

June
Lee moves north into Pennsylvania

June 28
General Meade replaces Hooker

July 1–3
Battle of Gettysburg

I have heard . . . of your recently saying that both the Army and the Government needed a Dictator. . . . Only those generals who gain successes, can set up dictators. What I now ask of you is military success, and I will risk the dictatorship.

—Abraham Lincoln to General Joseph Hooker, January 26, 1863

> *Beware of rashness, but with energy and sleepless vigilance go forward and give us victories.*
>
> —President Abraham Lincoln to Major General Joseph Hooker, January 26, 1863

Hooker replaced him. Hooker was a West Point graduate from the Class of 1837. Like many other Civil War generals, he had served in the war against Mexico. By January 1863, he was known to be a strong, able leader. His nickname was "Fighting Joe."

Hooker was popular with the men he commanded. He was able to organize and boost the morale of a discouraged army. On the other hand, his lifestyle and morals were less correct. He had **schemed** to replace Burnside, his commanding officer. He had publically suggested that the country needed a dictator. Furthermore, his camp was known for excessive drinking and other bad behaviors.

> *The hen is the wisest of all the animal creation because she never cackles until the egg is laid.*
>
> —Abraham Lincoln about Hooker's plans

When he appointed Hooker to command, Lincoln cautioned the general to provide solid action instead of boasts. Hooker began planning the great victory he had promised. Lincoln needed the political boost a victory would bring, and Hooker was confident he could deliver.

The Battle of Chancellorsville

Following the Battle of Fredericksburg, Lee's troops expanded and improved their network of trenches around Fredericksburg. Hooker made plans to avoid this strongly fortified location. Instead, he would cross the Rappahannock and head south to come around Lee's army and cut the supply lines. The idea was sound but Hooker, like previous generals, was **inadequate** to the task.

> *My plans are perfect, and when I start to carry them out, may God have mercy on Bobby Lee, for I shall have none.*
>
> —Major General Joseph Hooker, April 12, 1863

What Do You Know!

The job of the cavalry (horse-mounted soldiers) was crucial. Information on the enemy was gained through scouting expeditions. The cavalry also raided supply lines and pursued fleeing foot soldiers. The cavalry patrolled around its army to prevent surprise attacks from the enemy.

In late April, according to plan, the main portion of Hooker's army crossed the river. These 70,000 men were to march around Lee's forces. Another 40,000 under the command of Major General John Sedgwick, a West Point classmate of Hooker, crossed the river near Fredericksburg. Their job was to draw Lee's attention while the greater force moved around behind him.

Hooker Changes the Plan

All was going according to plan on April 30. Then, believing his troops to be outnumbered, Hooker stopped his offense. Instead of completing the trap around Lee, he stopped and positioned his army at Chancellorsville, 9 miles (14 km) west of Fredericksburg.

Chancellorsville was not a town. It was a tavern surrounded by several smaller buildings. It was built at the intersection of two main roads. Here Hooker abandoned his advantage and halted his forces to wait for reinforcements. The officers under him were shocked, discouraged, and confused.

General Stonewall Jackson leading Confederate troops at the Battle of Chancellorsville

Jackson's Plan

Lee was quick to take advantage of Hooker's mistake. He moved his forces into position to attack Hooker at Chancellorsville. Meanwhile, General T.J. "Stonewall" Jackson prepared for a daring maneuver that would complete the Union disaster. A local guide led Jackson and his men through the backcountry of the Virginia Wilderness. In the afternoon of May 2, Jackson was in a position to attack the Union army from behind its lines.

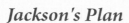

To hear from his own lip that the advantages gained by the successful marches of his lieutenants were to culminate in fighting a defensive battle in that next of thickets was too much, and I retired from his presence with the belief that my commanding general was a whipped man.

—Major General Darius N. Couch, about General Hooker after the march to Chancellorsville

People in the War

Major John Sedgwick

John Sedgwick was an able artillery officer and a veteran of the Seminole and Mexican-American Wars. He commanded divisions in numerous battles in the Civil War. On May 9, 1864, at the battle of Spotsylvania Courthouse, he directed placement of artillery. To calm the soldiers' skittishness about Confederate bullets, he commented to his men, "They couldn't hit an elephant at this distance." Within moments, he was killed by a Confederate sniper.

> *He has lost his left arm; but I have lost my right arm.*
>
> —Robert E. Lee, about Stonewall Jackson

The battle hung in the balance for a time, but excellent leadership by Southern generals matched the North's superiority of numbers. Hooker did not use his advantages and even surrendered strong positions for no clear reason. He ordered a corps positioned on high ground to fall back from its strong position. Lee's men promptly took over Hazel Grove and two previously separated portions of the army were rejoined. Confederate artillery placed there was able to fire into the Union defenses around Chancellorsville.

In the fighting at nearby Fredericksburg, Major General John Sedgwick and his men were able to make costly progress against Lee's men. Lee quickly reinforced his weakened lines at Fredericksburg, however, and gained the upper hand there, too. Instead of attacking Lee's lines where they were depleted by reinforcements sent to Fredericksburg, Hooker gave up and withdrew. Sedgwick had no option but to follow his commanding officer in retreat.

The Result

The Army of the Potomac retreated across the Rappahannock River under cover of darkness on the night of May 5. With the withdrawal of Union forces, Lee was denied a decisive and complete victory. Still, it was a crushing defeat for the Union.

When the dust of the battle settled, it became clear that the Battle of Chancellorsville was full of **paradoxes**. The largest Union army assembled during the war, 130,000 men, was defeated by a force half its size. Lee's army numbered only 60,000. Union forces lost 17,000 men to Lee's loss of 13,000. By percentages, however, the Confederate losses were far worse. Twenty-two percent of Lee's army were killed or injured at Chancellorsville compared to fifteen percent of the Union army.

The great Confederate victory was also a great Confederate loss. Even worse, Lee lost one of his most beloved and daring generals. The evening of May 2, Stonewall Jackson rode out to see where Union troops were located to plan a renewed attack. On his return to the Confederate line, he was shot in the left arm by his own troops. His shattered arm was amputated, but he died eight days later. His loss was keenly felt by Lee and the Confederate army.

In spite of the Confederate losses, the Battle of Chancellorsville was a high point for the Confederacy and for General Lee. Lee's army regarded him with an awe approaching worship. Many called the battle Lee's greatest victory. For Lincoln and the Union, it marked a point of deep discouragement and low **morale**. Many believed that the war was lost and Lincoln was to blame.

My God! My God! What will the country say?

—Abraham Lincoln, after the Union defeat at Chancellorsville

The Battle of Gettysburg

Just two months after the defeat at Chancellorsville, the Union's Army of the Potomac achieved a stunning victory at Gettysburg, Pennsylvania. This was a victory for both military and political reasons.

The Road from Chancellorsville

Following his victory at Chancellorsville, Lee wanted to seize the momentum and move into Union territory. He believed that another stunning win, this time on Union soil, would shatter the resolve of the enemy. It also would provide political benefits for the Confederacy.

The time seemed ripe for this plan. Lincoln's popularity was very low. His political opponents in the North believed that Chancellorsville proved that war could never restore the Union. In the meantime, as more men were needed to fight the seemingly endless war, Congress had authorized a very unpopular draft. Lee thought a Confederate victory, combined with discontent on the home front, would cripple the Union.

Jefferson Davis, president of the Confederacy, was not convinced that the time was right for Lee's proposal. He and others in his Cabinet were concerned by the events in Mississippi. By this time, Grant's activities were a real threat to Vicksburg and Confederate control of the Mississippi River (see Chapter 4). Davis proposed sending some of Lee's men to Mississippi to fight for Vicksburg.

Lee argued his point personally. It would take weeks for troops to reach Mississippi. Vicksburg would stand or fall before they could arrive. The troops could be used far more effectively in the Eastern Theater. His proposed invasion of Pennsylvania would have a great emotional impact by crushing the Union on its own soil. It would also relieve the strain on the Virginia countryside by moving the

What Do You Know!

Many important Civil War generals were in the West Point Class of 1837. Besides Joseph Hooker and John Sedgwick, this class included Braxton Bragg, who led the Army of Tennessee, Jubal Early, who unsuccessfully defended Marye's Heights against Sedgwick on May 3, 1863, and John C. Pemberton, who was a West Point roommate of George Meade.

People in the War

John Ewell Brown "Jeb" Stuart

One of the South's most famous Cavalry officers was James Ewell Brown "Jeb" Stuart. He was a dashing, bold, and skilled leader. He excelled at discovering the strength and location of the enemy. He led the cavalry (horse-mounted troops) of the Army of Northern Virginia in many important battles such as Seven Days, Second Manassas, Antietam, Fredericksburg, and Gettysburg. He took over Stonewall Jackson's command after Jackson was killed at Chancellorsville. Stuart was killed in battle outside Richmond, Virginia, in May 1864.

Confederate army to well-stocked land untouched by war. In addition, a Confederate victory at this point would sway foreign countries into finally recognizing the Confederacy as a nation. And finally, this victory would naturally relieve the pressure on Vicksburg because the Union army in the West would be forced to march to the defense of the East.

Lee Moves North

Lee's arguments won the day. He received permission to move forward with his plan. He reorganized his army and placed Jackson's men, who had lost their general at Chancellorsville, under new leadership. The Army of Northern Virginia was also restocked and resupplied. The men were encouraged. Nevertheless, the drive into Pennsylvania was a great opportunity to seize badly needed supplies for the army. As Lee's army passed through northern territory, raiding parties brought in clothing, shoes, and food. In fact, the location of the great battle at Gettysburg was actually the result of a quest for supplies.

The Armies Meet at Gettysburg

It was reported that a large stockpile of shoes could be found at Gettysburg, a town located at the **junction** of several main roads in Pennsylvania. A Confederate division was authorized to go to Gettysburg and secure the shoes.

In the meantime, the Union army had been undergoing changes. President Lincoln had pressured General Hooker to move forward and attack Lee before the Army of Northern Virginia could cross the Potomac. Hooker, like McClellan before him, was slow to move. On June 28, 1863, Lincoln replaced Hooker with General George Gordon Meade. Another West Point graduate, Meade had worked his way up through the ranks but was not well known.

At this point, however, Meade had something Lee did not have: knowledge of the enemy's position. One of the most vital jobs of

If I had had Stonewall Jackson with me, so far as man can see, I should have won the battle of Gettysburg.

—Robert E. Lee

> *General Stuart, where have you been? I have not heard a word from you in days, and you the eyes and ears of my army.*
>
> —Robert E. Lee, to Jeb Stuart, July 2, 1863

General George Meade

the cavalry was to gather information on the location and activities of enemy forces. Jeb Stuart was Lee's eyes and ears, bringing him information on enemy activities. Unfortunately for Lee, Stuart had become separated from the rest of the Confederate army, effectively "blinding" Lee to Union troop movements. Meade, on the other hand, had excellent information from his cavalry. Unlike previous generals, he was not slow to act on his information.

The location of Gettysburg was important. It was at the junction of several important roads. It was surrounded by ridges and hills. From a military standpoint, defense of this high ground would be important in a battle. The Confederate army's control of the hills and ridges had helped win the day at Fredericksburg.

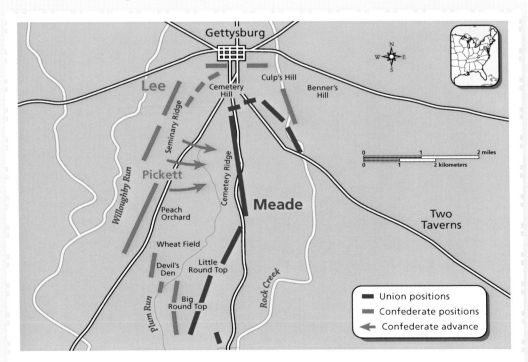

Battle of Gettysburg, July 3 (Day 3)

The Battle

DAY ONE When the Confederate forces sent to Gettysburg for supplies arrived on the morning of July 1, they discovered that the Union had arrived first. Two brigades of Union cavalry already occupied defensible ground northwest of the town. The two forces immediately clashed and each side called for reinforcements. The hard-pressed defenders fell back to Cemetery Hill. Lee arrived and ordered Ewell, who had replaced Jackson, to advance if possible. Where Jackson would have attacked and produced a great victory, Ewell chose caution and stayed put.

As evening fell on July 1, Union forces commanded the hills around Gettysburg. They began to fortify their positions. In the meantime, the bulk of the Union army, drawn by the sound of gunfire, had hurried to reinforce the defenders.

At the battle of Gettysburg, both the North and South used different tactics than in previous battles. Northern armies had been hampered by poor leadership. Generals had failed to move up reinforcements where needed and had wasted lives by throwing men against strong fortifications. At Gettysburg, the Union lines were arranged in a manner that made it practical to shift troops here and there to quickly replace and reinforce weak spots. Union generals spotted weak points in the lines and filled them before Confederate forces broke through.

Pickett's Charge at the Battle of Gettysburg

DAY TWO On July 2, the second day of the battle, Lee ordered an assault on the Union's defenses. Against the odds, exhausted Union regiments held their positions against strong assaults. This time Southern leadership was lacking, as generals failed to move quickly and missed opportunities. Lee himself was ill and his usual quick understanding of the military situation lagged. At the end of battle that day, the Confederate forces had failed to drive out the Union defenders at Gettysburg.

DAY THREE On July 3, Lee planned an all-out offensive against Union positions. When General Longstreet urged caution because of the strong union fortifications, Lee insisted that his men could accomplish what others could not.

Soldiers' National Cemetery at Gettysburg

To prepare for the assault, Confederate artillery battered the Union lines for nearly two hours. However, their aim was high. After a time, the Union artillery commander ordered the big guns to stop firing, causing the Confederates to believe that they had been destroyed. There followed one of the most memorable moments of Gettysburg, often called Pickett's Charge.

Nine divisions charged across the farmland. Suddenly, the Union artillery burst out with proof that the guns were not destroyed. At 200 yards (183 m), Union soldiers began firing. When it was over, and the Confederate survivors had struggled back to their lines, nearly half of the original 14,000 had fallen or been captured. Lee recognized defeat and withdrew in a heavy rainstorm on July 4. Meade, unsure of Lee's strength, did not pursue him.

On the battlefield at Gettysburg, both armies lost staggering numbers of men. It had been the bloodiest battle of the Civil War. The Union suffered 23,000 casualties, more than one-fourth of the army. Confederate losses were 28,000 men killed, wounded, or missing. This represented about one-third of Lee's forces. In his retreat, Lee left 7,000 wounded soldiers to the care of Union surgeons and nurses.

The Gettysburg Address

On November 19, 1863, President Lincoln spoke at the dedication of a cemetery for Union soldiers who had died at Gettysburg. His address became one of the best-known speeches of all time. In his speech, he reminded his listeners that the war was not over and that it was the responsibility of the living to complete the work of those who had died.

> *That we here highly resolve these dead shall not have died in vain; that the nation, shall have a new birth of freedom, and that government of the people by the people for the people, shall not perish from the earth.*
>
> —Abraham Lincoln, November 19, 1863

Turning Points in the Eastern Theater

In spite of the staggering losses there, Gettysburg was an important victory for the Union. If the Union had lost, France and England would probably have offered aid to the Confederacy. Lincoln would have faced severe pressure from political enemies within the Union. Instead, any hopes the Confederacy had for foreign **intervention** were ended. In addition, the South had made two attempts to push the war onto Union territory. Both had failed. The rest of the war would be fought on Southern soil.

At the same time that the Union cheered this turning point victory, news of another great victory reached Washington. The day after the Battle of Gettysburg ended, the Union had won another turning point battle in the West at Vicksburg.

Lincoln's address at the dedication of the Soldiers' National Cemetery at Gettysburg, November 19, 1863

4 *Vicksburg*

The Civil War was not just an Eastern conflict. In the West, Union and Confederate forces clashed in battles along the major rivers and in the interior of Kentucky and Tennessee.

The Anaconda Plan

When the Civil War began, General Winfield Scott proposed a plan to cut off the South from its supplies. Invading the South, he argued, would be too expensive. Instead, the Union should use its navy to surround the South.

Scott proposed that the Union navy **blockade** Southern ports and that gunboats patrol the Mississippi River. Since the South needed to sell cotton in Europe to buy ships, arms, food, and other supplies, a successful blockade would strangle the Confederacy. Newspapers quickly labeled this the "**Anaconda Plan**" and pictured it as a giant snake circling and squeezing the life out of the South.

The Union navy began a blockade in the early months of the war. With 3,500 miles (5,633 km) of coastline to patrol, it was a huge task.

Vicksburg is the key. The war can never be brought to a close until the key is in our pocket. We can take all the northern parts of the Confederacy, and they still can defy us from Vicksburg.

—Abraham Lincoln

Major Events

1862

December
Grant's first attempt to take Vicksburg fails

1863

April 16 & 22
Gunboats and transports pass Vicksburg

May 19 & 22
Grant tries to take Vicksburg but fails

May–July
Siege of Vicksburg

July 4
Surrender of Vicksburg

People in the War

General John Eaton

In November 1862, General Grant appointed John Eaton, an army chaplain, as superintendent of contraband (newly freed slaves) for the Mississippi Valley. Eaton, an educator by training, organized the freedmen into camps and was responsible for providing them with food, education, and work. His organization provided the blueprint for the Freedmen's Bureau after the Civil War.

In the interior of the continent, the North controlled the Missouri and upper Mississippi Rivers. Cairo, at the junction of the Mississippi and Ohio Rivers, was in Illinois, a Union state. The lower Mississippi River was in Confederate hands. The South fortified key locations along the river to keep control of the lower Mississippi.

Ocean-going ships could not navigate the shallower waters of the inland rivers. Therefore, the Union navy designed a fleet of shallow-draft, flat-bottomed vessels loaded with guns. The gunboats had paddle wheels, guns, and iron armor. This armor, designed by Samuel Pook, reminded people of turtle shells so the boats were nicknamed "Pook's turtles."

With the fall of New Orleans and Memphis in late April and early June 1862, most of the Mississippi River came under Union control. Only a 240-mile section (386 km) between Vicksburg and Port Hudson resisted Union control. Capturing Vicksburg was the key to gaining Union control of the Mississippi River.

Vicksburg's location made it a difficult site to conquer. It was a fortified city located at the top of a 200-foot (61 m) **bluff**. No river traffic could move past Vicksburg without coming under fire from the guns located on the sides and top of the cliff. To attack the city from the river would require scaling the sides of the bluff under fire, a nearly impossible task. To attack by land would mean crossing through land held by the Confederate army.

Vicksburg Winter Battles

The task of conquering Vicksburg was given to General Ulysses S. Grant. He first attempted to take the city in December 1862. He planned to approach the city from two directions. General Sherman, setting out from Memphis, would travel down the Mississippi and approach Vicksburg from the north. Grant would travel south through Confederate territory. This two-pronged approach would divide the attention of Confederate forces.

> *In my opinion, the opening of the Mississippi River will be to us of more advantage than the capture of forty Richmonds.*
>
> —General Halleck, to General Grant, March 20, 1863

Confederate cavalry raiders, who cut his supply line on December 20, foiled General Grant's plan. Grant was forced to call off the campaign and withdraw his forces through enemy territory. His men survived by raiding the surrounding countryside for food for themselves and their horses. This experience taught Grant that his army could travel without depending on a supply line if necessary.

Grant and Sherman could not communicate when Confederate raiders destroyed several miles (km) of railroad and telegraph lines. This prevented Grant from informing Sherman that he had cancelled the attack on Vicksburg.

Unaware of Grant's withdrawal, Sherman left Memphis the same day that Grant's supply line was severed. He took his men to a point north of Vicksburg. On December 29, 1862, Sherman's forces crossed Chickasaw Bayou to attack Vicksburg. Since Grant's army was not in place to distract the defenders of Vicksburg, the full power of the city's guns was turned on Sherman's force. After losing nearly 1,800 men, Sherman withdrew. Confederate forces lost 200 men. The winter assault on Vicksburg had failed.

Grant used newly freed slaves from nearby plantations to help dig the canal at Vicksburg.

More Attempts to Reach Vicksburg

During the next several months, Grant occupied his army with different approaches to Vicksburg. The Mississippi River makes a sharp bend near Vicksburg. A canal southwest across the land at the mouth of this bend was already begun. During the winter months, Grant kept his men busy trying to widen and deepen this trench so the gunboats and transports could pass through it. This plan was swamped when a dam broke and flooded the canal.

Three other attempts to bring men and boats from upriver also met with failure. A water passage from an area called Lake Providence could not provide access quickly enough for a large force. Passages through the swampy land around the Yazoo River were made difficult by the overhanging trees. In addition, Confederates blocked the narrow streams with trees to slow Union progress. Finally, Grant returned to plans for a land and water assault similar to the one that had failed in December.

The plan Grant proposed was so daring that many of his staff, including Sherman, objected. Grant considered the importance of Vicksburg worth the risk. Phase 1 began on the moonless night of April 16, 1863. Several gunboats and three transports moved past the Confederate guns at Vicksburg. The big guns sank only one of the transport ships. The remaining boats took up a position downriver. On the night of April 22, 13 more Union boats ran past the Confederate batteries at Vicksburg. One transport and six barges were sunk, but the rest joined the boats that had come through earlier. Grant now had two of his three Army Corps in a position 30 miles (48 km) south of Vicksburg, and he had a fleet of transport boats to move them across the river.

Vicksburg Summer Battles

On May 1, General Grant began to move his men across the river to Confederate territory. Grant planned two **distractions** to keep the Confederates busy while his men crossed the river. The first distraction was provided by Benjamin Grierson and the 1,700 men in his cavalry brigade. During the last two weeks of April, they dashed through central Mississippi, tearing up rail lines that supplied Vicksburg. Many of the troops under Confederate General John C. Pemberton, which would have been defending Vicksburg, were off chasing Grierson.

🌠 What Do You Know!

Both the North and the South developed ram ships for river warfare. Rams were heavy, powered vessels with a heavy, reinforced metal bow. The ram ship would slam into the hull of an enemy ship to damage or sink it. In March 1862, the U.S. Army authorized the construction of a fleet of ram ships built by Charles Ellet, a civil engineer.

Union ships running the Confederate blockade on the Mississippi River at Vicksburg

A second distraction was provided by General Sherman. He returned to the Chickasaw Bayou, scene of his bloody defeat in December 1862. There Sherman pretended to prepare for an assault on the city. For two days, his men made it look as though they meant to attack. For good measure, the navy shelled the city. As a result, soldiers who had been on their way to challenge Grant at his river crossing were called back to defend the city.

Port Gibson

Once across the river, Grant needed to take Port Gibson to secure his position. This was quickly done. When Port Gibson was reinforced as a supply base, Grant moved east instead of west. He reasoned that it would be better to defeat the forces at Jackson before moving on Vicksburg. That way, he would not need to worry about being caught between two enemy forces.

Grant had learned in December that his army could live off the land. This allowed his men to move more quickly. Without the **hindrance** of maintaining a supply line, Grant marched east toward Jackson, Mississippi, where Confederate General Joseph Johnston was organizing his troops to move against Grant.

Points East and Vicksburg

During the next two weeks, Grant swept east. On May 12, he defeated the Confederate forces at the town of Raymond and then continued on to Jackson. On May 14, he overran the Confederate defenses at Jackson and took that city. Leaving Sherman to destroy rail lines and supplies, Grant turned to head back west.

While Johnston and Pemberton discussed tactics, Grant defeated Pemberton's forces at the Battle of Champion's Hill on May 16.

> *The enemy is badly beaten, greatly demoralized, and exhausted of ammunition. The road to Vicksburg is open. All we want now are men, ammunition, and hard bread. We can subsist our horses on the country, and obtain considerable supplies for our troops.*
>
> —Ulysses S. Grant, to William T. Sherman, May 3, 1863

What Do You Know!

Contraband was the term used for Southern slaves who escaped to the Union army. Many of these African Americans fought in the Union army in the West. Two regiments of contraband defended a Union garrison at Milliken's Bend just upriver from Vicksburg during the siege of Vicksburg.

The Confederates fell back to Big Black River, where they were defeated on May 17. The remaining Confederate soldiers retreated into Vicksburg. On May 17, Grant was at Vicksburg. He tried to take the town, but attempts on May 19 and 22 both failed. The Confederates may have retreated, but they were still able to fight.

The Siege of Vicksburg

Although he had been unable to take the town by assault, Grant was in the position to take it by siege. For six weeks, his troops kept Vicksburg's defenders trapped inside their fortifications. As supplies ran low, Pemberton asked for help from Confederate troops in the East. General Lee, however, argued successfully that his plan to attack the Union in Pennsylvania would be the best way of helping Vicksburg's defenders.

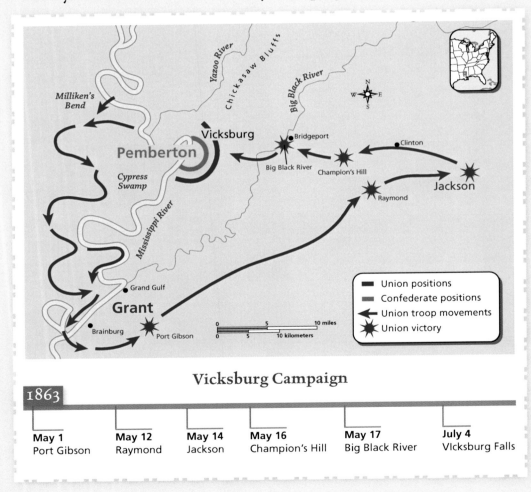

Vicksburg Campaign

1863					
May 1 Port Gibson	**May 12** Raymond	**May 14** Jackson	**May 16** Champion's Hill	**May 17** Big Black River	**July 4** Vicksburg Falls

> *Until this moment I never thought your expedition a success.*
> *I never could see the end clearly until now. But this is a*
> *campaign. This is a success if we never take the town.*
>
> —William T. Sherman, to Ulysses Grant, May 17, 1863

Ironically, the surrender of Confederate troops at Vicksburg came on July 4, 1863. General Pemberton realized that his sick and starving men could hold out no longer, and he agreed to surrender the fort. At the same time, in the East, Confederate forces were retreating from their defeat at Gettysburg. News of the fall of Vicksburg came hard on the heels of the Gettysburg victory. The two events, both on the celebration of the nation's Independence Day, were a huge encouragement and morale boost to the Union.

Port Hudson and Milliken's Bend

While Grant was **besieging** Vicksburg, Nathaniel Banks was doing the same to Port Hudson to the south. He had laid siege to that fort in late May through June, making two unsuccessful assaults on May 27 and June 14. Two Union regiments of African Americans fought bravely at Port Hudson, impressing Union officers, soldiers, and the public with their courage. "The severe test to which they were subjected, and the determined manner in which they encountered the enemy, leaves upon my mind no doubt of their ultimate success," Banks reported.

It was at Milliken's Bend, however, that Southern outrage at arming former slaves boiled over into one of the bloodiest battles of the Civil War. The Confederate troops attacked the garrison there, hoping to break Grant's supply line and relieve Vicksburg. With their backs to the Mississippi River, several Union African–American regiments fought alongside a few white regiments. The fighting was fierce, with soldiers using **bayonets** and rifle butts in hand-to-hand combat. Navy gunboats came to the aid of the Union troops. Their line held, but at a cost. African–American troops suffered heavy losses, with the 9th Louisiana Infantry losing almost half of its men. Most captured African–American soldiers were

 **What Do You Know!**

John C. Pemberton, was the Confederate general in command at Vicksburg. He was a former classmate of Ulysses S. Grant at West Point. Pemberton thought he could get more favorable terms of surrender on the patriotic holiday of July 4. Grant's reply to Pemberton's proposal earned him the nickname "Unconditional Surrender Grant." In reality, the North could not afford to take 30,000 prisoners. The Confederates were released on parole. They had to promise to go home and stop fighting.

executed, which was against the rules of war, and some were sold into slavery.

With news of the surrender of Vicksburg, Confederates at Port Hudson gave up. They surrendered on July 9. The entire Mississippi River was under Union control. With the blockade of the Confederate coast, the South was encircled. The Anaconda Plan was complete. The Union could begin to squeeze the South.

> *Good Heavens! Are these the long-boasted fortifications of Vicksburg? It was the rebels, and not their works, that kept us out of the city.*
>
> —Union General James McPherson, July 4, 1863

The Loss of Vicksburg

The Confederate loss of Vicksburg and Port Hudson were important turning points in the Civil War. The morale of the Union received a huge boost. The Mississippi River was now a Union-controlled river. The South was on the run, it seemed, in the West.

Confederate President Jefferson Davis blamed the loss of Vicksburg on General Johnston. Not only had Johnston failed to relieve the besieged city but he had also withdrawn his army, abandoning much of the West to Union troops. In the West, Vicksburg and Grant had turned the tide. The Union was advancing, and the South was retreating.

> *This is a day of jubilee, a day of rejoicing to the faithful. . . . Already are my orders out to give one big huzza and sling the knapsack for new fields.*
>
> —General Sherman, to General Grant, regarding the victory at Vicksburg

5 Chickamauga and Chattanooga

I n December of 1862, Grant and Sherman were failing in their first attempt to take Vicksburg. The Army of the Potomac was retreating from the loss at Fredericksburg. In Tennessee, General William S. Rosecrans, commander of the Union Army of the Cumberland, was preparing to take his troops into battle.

Stones River to Chickamauga

Although Lincoln had strongly urged him to move sooner, Rosecrans's forces did not leave Nashville until the day after Christmas. Confederate cavalry harassed them but did not stop their march. On December 30, Rosecrans and his men came up against the Confederate army under the command of General Braxton Bragg. The Confederate forces occupied ground on both sides of the Stones River, about 2 miles (3 km) northwest of Murfreesboro. That night, men who would fight one another to the death the following day, joined together in singing "Home Sweet Home" across the picket lines.

Major Events

1862

December 31–
January 2
Battle of Stones
River

1863

June 24
Rosecrans begins
Tullahoma
Campaign

September 19–20
Battle of
Chickamauga

September 21–
November 25
Siege of
Chattanooga

November 23–25
Battle for
Chattanooga

General
Braxton Bragg

General William
Rosecrans

The Confederates attacked early in the morning, while Union soldiers were still eating breakfast. Caught off guard, the Union troops were unable to stop the enemy's advance. The Confederates pushed forward until they came up against the men of Union General Philip Sheridan. He had anticipated trouble and wakened his men early. Although they took heavy losses, Sheridan's men slowed the Confederate advance. The Union line was pushed back into a wooded area called the Round Forest. There the Union soldiers dug in and held their place.

That night, as the old year ended, Bragg was so confident of success that he cabled news of his victory to the authorities in Richmond. The Union army, he assured them, was retreating. Far from retreating, however, Union soldiers proceeded to capture a hill on the other side of the river the next day.

On January 2, Bragg ordered a division to retake this hill. Union artillery helped to shatter the attack. Bragg realized he would not win, so he retreated the following night. Rosecrans, his army badly battered, did not follow. Though costly to both sides, the battle was a Union victory.

Chickamauga to Chattanooga (Tullahoma Campaign)

Following the Battle of Stones River, Rosecrans spent six months reorganizing his army and repairing his communication and supply lines. President Lincoln pushed him to move against General Bragg's Army of Tennessee when Grant moved against Vicksburg. Rosecrans, however, insisted in May that his army was not yet prepared.

"
You do not appear to observe the fact that this noble army has driven the rebels from Middle Tennessee . . . I beg in behalf of this army that the War Department may not overlook so great an event because it is not written in letters of blood.

—William B. Rosecrans, to the Secretary of War
"

On June 24, 1863, Rosecrans was ready to lead his Union Army of the Cumberland against the Confederate Army of Tennessee. His careful planning paid off. He came at the Confederates from both sides in the Duck River valley, forcing Bragg to withdraw. Rosecrans pursued and, by the beginning of July, Bragg was falling back to Chattanooga. In just over a week, Rosecrans had driven the Army of Tennessee 80 miles (129 km), nearly to Georgia, with only 570 casualties. After the **horrific** loss of life at Gettysburg and Vicksburg, these numbers were particularly impressive.

The Battle of Chickamauga

After another pause to regroup and restore his communication and supply lines, Rosecrans marched again on August 16. His goal now was the important rail line linking Chattanooga to Atlanta. In the meantime, General Burnside occupied Knoxville on September 3. Confederate forces fled from Knoxville and joined Bragg near Chattanooga. This was a low point for the Confederate army in Tennessee. Low morale and troop desertions plagued Bragg. Jefferson Davis, fearful of losing this crucial territory, sent reinforcements to Bragg and instructed him to take the offensive.

Bragg attempted to trick Rosecrans into an ambush by providing "**disinformation**." Men who pretended to be Confederate deserters informed the Union army that their army was retreating. When Rosecrans moved to follow without sufficient scouting, Bragg ordered his subordinates to attack. The plan failed because Bragg's generals distrusted him and did not attack. Instead of being ambushed, Rosecrans was able to establish his army in the valley of the West Chickamauga Creek.

Rosecrans's position by the West Chickamauga was reinforced by troops under General George Thomas. Battle between Union and Confederate forces began at dawn on September 19. Bragg launched continual attacks against Thomas's position but failed to break the line. Thomas was forced back slowly, fighting hard. Both sides paid in blood for each foot of ground the Union lost.

Defeat at Chickamauga

The battle continued the next day, September 20. Late that morning Confederate General Longstreet, who had brought forces out from Virginia to reinforce Bragg's Army of Tennessee, ordered his soldiers to

People in the War

General James Longstreet

Confederate General James Longstreet graduated from West Point in the Class of 1842, along with Union generals William Rosecrans and John Pope. One of his best friends was Ulysses S. Grant, who graduated the following year. Following the Civil War, Longstreet became a Republican and supported Grant for the presidency. He further infuriated fellow Southerners by criticizing Robert E. Lee's leadership. When he died in 1904, Longstreet had managed to outlive almost all of his critics.

Battle of Chickamauga, September 19–20, 1863

charge the Union position. By chance, his attack hit just as Rosecrans was shifting troops to fill a supposed gap on the line. Longstreet's men broke through the weakened Union point. The momentum of their charge carried them all the way to Rosecrans's headquarters. Union soldiers, including Rosecrans and several of his generals, fled in panic to Chattanooga.

General Thomas was left to hold the field, which he did ably. He regrouped the remaining two-thirds of the Union army and was reinforced by General Gordon Granger, who brought up the reserve division from the rear. The reorganized Union soldiers held their position until nightfall. Then they retreated to Chattanooga, but in a more organized manner than the mid-day **rout**. For his stand that day, Thomas gained the nickname, "the Rock of Chickamauga."

Chattanooga

Longstreet urged Bragg to pursue the retreating Union army immediately. If he had, the Army of Tennessee might have scored a real victory. Bragg was concerned, however, about the state of his men. The Union troops had retreated, but Bragg had lost almost 30 percent of his available fighting men. Ten of his generals had been killed or wounded. Deeply shocked by his losses, he paused to rest and reorganize his troops.

The Union army, those who had fled and those who had retreated in an orderly fashion, had time to prepare their defenses in Chattanooga. Bragg prepared to lay siege to the town. He placed artillery on Lookout Mountain and infantry on Missionary Ridge and other roads into Chattanooga. The town was also cut off from the rail line. A road lay open through the Cumberland Mountains to the north, but the route was so difficult that very few supplies could be brought in that way. Bragg was confident that he could starve the Union defenders into surrender.

Although still in command in Chattanooga, Rosecrans seemed unable to take charge. While the Army of Cumberland was reduced to half rations and less, President Lincoln prepared to act on their behalf. First, to turn the military situation over to General Grant, he created a new division—the Division of Mississippi. Grant was placed in charge of this. Rosecrans was relieved of command and replaced by General Thomas. Reinforcements, under the command of General Joe Hooker were sent from Virginia.

He is confused and stunned, like a duck hit on the head, ever since Chickamauga.

—President Lincoln, about General Rosecrans

People in the War

General George Thomas

A native Virginian whose family owned slaves, Thomas graduated from West Point in 1840. Serving in artillery and cavalry units, Thomas taught both subjects at West Point. When the Civil War began, Thomas refused a commission in the Confederate army. His former student Jeb Stuart was so angry at Thomas for remaining with the Union that he wanted to "hang him as a traitor to his native state." Thomas's Southern family disowned him.

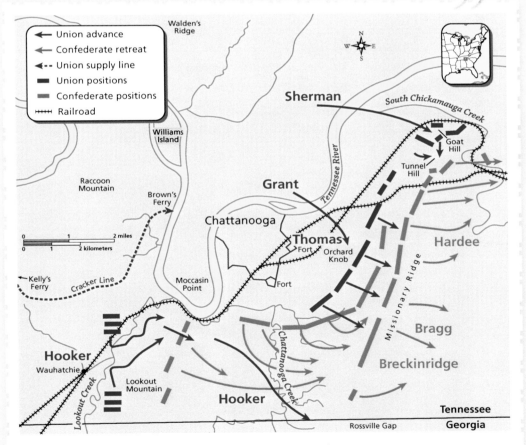

Chattanooga Campaign, November 24–25, 1863

Breaking the Siege

The Confederate army under Bragg still held positions on Lookout Mountain and Missionary Ridge. President Davis, however, took away more than one-quarter of Bragg's forces. Davis sent Longstreet and his 15,000 men to retake Knoxville. This decision resulted in a double loss, as not only did the Confederates fail to retake Knoxville but it also deprived Bragg of the forces he needed to hold Chattanooga.

Grant arrived at Chattanooga October 23 to take personal command of the situation. Within a week, he had opened the way for supplies to enter the besieged town, dubbed the "Cracker Line." With food for the defenders of Chattanooga, Grant was ready to lay his battle plans.

The Battle

By mid-November, Grant had his army in place to move into battle. Hooker had arrived with 20,000 men from the Army of the Potomac. Sherman brought in another 17,000 men, and Thomas had 35,000 men in his army. Grant was concerned that Thomas's men, who had been besieged in Chattanooga for weeks, might be too discouraged to fight well. Grant planned to use Sherman's and Hooker's soldiers for most of the fighting. Thomas's men could hold a position near Missionary Ridge and provide a threat to the Confederate position.

The Confederates had used the previous two months to build a series of three parallel trench lines along the base, middle, and top of Missionary Ridge. Grant thought that a direct assault on Missionary Ridge would be useless and wasteful. Instead, he proposed to attack both ends of the Confederate line. Hooker would take Lookout Mountain, while Sherman moved against the northeastern end of the line.

Battle of Lookout Mountain, November 24, 1863

> ### What Do You Know!
>
> There were four varieties of artillery projectiles. *Solid shot* was a heavy, solid, cast-iron ball. *Shells* were hollow balls filled with gunpowder that exploded to produce a shower of sharp fragments. *Case shot* was a thin-walled ball packed with smaller iron or lead balls. *Canister*, a cylinder filled with small lead balls packed in sawdust, turned the artillery piece into a huge shotgun.

Battle of
Missionary Ridge,
November 25,
1863

The battle began in the early morning of November 23. General
Thomas's men attacked Confederate positions and took Orchard Knob.
The next day, General Hooker's men pushed their way up Lookout
Mountain. This has been called the "Battle Above the Clouds,"
because the mountain was wreathed in fog. Hooker's men drove
the Confederate defenders off the mountain. That night, Bragg
reorganized and concentrated his men on Missionary Ridge.

On November 25, Hooker and Sherman attacked each end of
Missionary Ridge. In the afternoon, Grant ordered Thomas to have his
men take some of the rifle trenches at the base of the ridge. Thomas's
men took the trenches. Then, instead of stopping, they charged on up
the slope, yelling "Chickamauga!" as a reminder of the bloody defeat
they wanted to avenge. The Confederate defenders were so surprised by
this frontal attack that they panicked and ran. Another turning point

*Brave men! You were ordered to go forward and take the rebel rifle-pits at
the foot of these hills; you did so; and then, by the Eternal! Without orders,
you pushed forward and took all the enemy's works on top!*

—Union General Wood, to his troops at Lookout Mountain, November 25, 1863

battle had been won by the Union armies. Chattanooga, the "Gateway to the Lower South" was in Union hands. This key city became the base for Sherman's famous March to the Sea in 1864.

Conclusion

In September 1862, the North was discouraged with the war. Northerners were debating how and whether to fight. The South, on the other hand, was riding a wave of victories. In the 15 months between September 1862 and November 1863, six significant battles became important turning points. By the end of November 1863, the tide had turned.

> *I am tired and sick of war. Its glory is all moonshine. It is only those who have neither fired a shot nor heard the shrieks and groans of the wounded who cry aloud for blood, for vengeance, for desolation. War is hell.*
>
> —William Tecumseh Sherman

The first turning point battle, the Union victory at Antietam, provided President Lincoln the opportunity he had been seeking to announce his Emancipation Proclamation. This was a turning point in the overall purpose of the war. From that moment on, it was a war to end slavery. The battles of Fredericksburg and Chancellorsville, although Confederate victories, were gained at great cost and weakened the South. Gettysburg and the fall of Vicksburg, great Union victories, ended attempts to carry the war into Northern territory and completed Union encirclement of the South. With the fall of Chattanooga, the Western entrance to the Confederacy was open. The South was losing the war.

In previous wars, citizens of the United States had banded together to fight a foreign enemy. In the Civil War, there was no foreign enemy. Americans fought each other. Such divisions do not heal easily.

Today, 150 years later, the pain of war has faded and these turning point battles hold a fascination for Americans. People study them, reenact them, and debate what would have happened if something had been done differently. The reality of this war, however, should not be forgotten. Close to 200,000 American soldiers lost their lives in just 15 months. The Civil War remains a tragedy in American history.

GLOSSARY

abolition The demand that slavery be ended in the United States

Anaconda Plan Union plan to defeat the Confederacy with a naval blockade of Southern seaports and by taking control of the Mississippi River

artillery Large guns that are usually mounted on a carriage so they can be moved from place to place and fired a long distance at enemy positions

bayonet A long knife that is attached to the end of an infantry rifle or musket for the purpose of close fighting with an enemy

besiege To surround and isolate a hostile city or town to deprive the people within it of food, water, and other essential supplies

blockade To use hostile ships to close off trade

bluff A high, vertical cliff that is difficult or impossible to climb

campaign A plan for military operations to accomplish specific goals

casualties A loss in the fighting strength of a military unit due to causes such as wounds or death

criticize To find fault with the thoughts or actions of another

disinformation Untrue information that is intended to confuse an enemy

distraction An action intended to draw the attention of an enemy

Emancipation Proclamation A proclamation made by President Abraham Lincoln that declared the slaves free in those areas of the Confederacy that were still fighting against the Union on January 1, 1863

forage To look for food and supplies often by looting the homes and farms of civilians

fortify To build barriers such as walls, earthworks, or trenches around a position for defensive purposes

hindrance Something that holds one back from accomplishing a goal; a restraint

horrific Something that is terrible, shocking, and horrifying

inadequate Unsuitable for a certain purpose

intervention To step in and help in the affairs of another

junction Location where several roads or railroads come together

mobilize To gather military forces together in preparation for war

momentum The ongoing motion or advancement of a object, person, or organization

morale The attitude of the troops

offensive The aggressive movement of troops as they attack an enemy

Glossary

paradox A thought, statement, or action that appears to be contradictory or absurd but really makes sense or is true

plunder To steal items such as food, horses, or valuables by force

principal Something that is first in order of importance

provisions Necessary items such as food and water

recruit A new member of a military unit

reinforcements Additional men and weapons that add strength to an existing military force

resources Sources of supplies

respond To act in response to the act of another

rout A disorganized retreat resulting from a military force being driven from its position by an enemy

scheme A plan for accomplishing a certain goal

secession The withdrawal of Southern states from the United States to set up a separate nation called the Confederate States of America

secure Safe; free from danger

sniper A rifleman who shoots at the enemy from a hidden position

strategist A person who makes plans for conducting warfare; that is, the movement of armed forces in relation to an enemy

sympathetic Concerned about the feelings or situation of another

MORE INFORMATION

Books

Elliot, Henry. *Frederick Douglass: From Slavery to Statesman.* Crabtree Publishing Company, 2010.

Foote, Shelby. *The Civil War: A Narrative.* (3 vols.) Random House, 1974.

Garrison, Webb. *Civil War Curiosities: Strange Stories, Oddities, Events, and Coincidences.* Rutledge Hill Press, 1994.

Massey, Mary Elizabeth. *Women in the Civil War.* University of Nebraska Press, 1994.

McPherson, James M. *The Illustrated Battle Cry of Freedom: The Civil War Era.* Oxford University Press, 2003.

Wagner, Margaret E. (ed.) *The Library of Congress Civil War Desk Reference.* Simon and Schuster, 2002.

Websites

www.pbs.org/civilwar
The Civil War/PBS. Companion site to Ken Burns's DVD *The Civil War.* Includes photos, maps, and video clips.

http://www.nps.gov/civilwar150/
National Park Service Website. In-depth articles, photos, and information on Civil War parks and park events.

www.civilwar.org/education/students/kidswebsites.html
Civil War Trust Websites for Kids. Has articles, photos, a glossary of Civil War terms, lists of books, and links to other websites.

www.civil-war.net
The Civil War Home Page. Has a photo gallery, lists of books and movies, battle maps, articles, diary excerpts, and reference materials.

http://www.archives.gov/research/military/civil-war/photos/index.html
The National Archives. Has pictures of the Civil War.

 About the Author

Sandra J. Hiller has a BA in History from the University of California, Santa Barbara, and an MA in History from the University of Texas, Permian Basin. Along with articles published in the Permian Historical Annual, she has written extensively for museum exhibits, newsletters, and textbook ancillaries.

INDEX